PIANO | VOCAL | GUITAR

JUSTIN BIEBER

T0066218

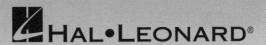

ISBN 978-1-70514-148-9

HAL•LEONARD®

Visit Hal Leonard Online at
www.halleonard.com

Contact us:
Hal Leonard
7777 West Bluemound Road
Milwaukee, WI 53213
Email: info@halleonard.com

In Europe, contact:
Hal Leonard Europe Limited
42 Wigmore Street
Marylebone, London, W1U 2RN
Email: info@halleonardeurope.com

In Australia, contact:
Hal Leonard Australia Pty. Ltd.
4 Lentara Court
Cheltenham, Victoria, 3192 Australia
Email: info@halleonard.com.au

CONTENTS

2 MUCH

Words and Music by JUSTIN BIEBER,
JOSHUA GUDWIN, SONNY MOORE,
ALEXANDER IZQUIERDO,GIAN STONE,
GREGORY HEIN, MARTIN LUTHER KING JR.
and FREDDY WEXLER

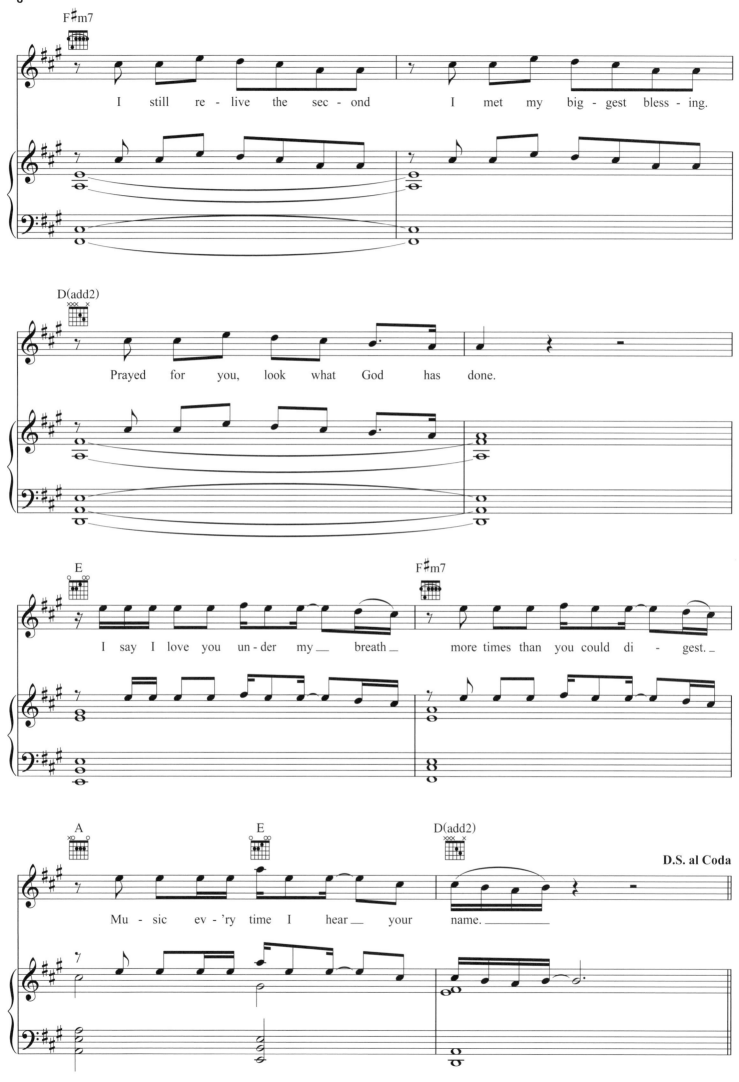

DESERVE YOU

Words and Music by JUSTIN BIEBER,
JONATHAN BELLION, LOUIS BELL,
ALI TAMPOSI, ANDREW WATT
and MICHAEL POLLACK

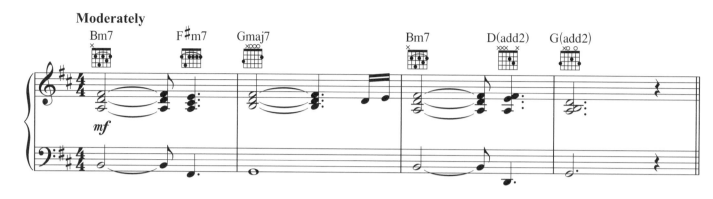

When I'm in my thoughts some-times, it's hard to be-lieve I'm the per-son you think I
I can tend to hold things back. ___ I need you more than I let you be-lieve I

am, the per-son that you tell me you love. ___
do, 'cause you could think it might be too much. ___ Oh ___ yeah. ___

I don't __ de - serve you __ to - night.

It's in the way that you hold me.

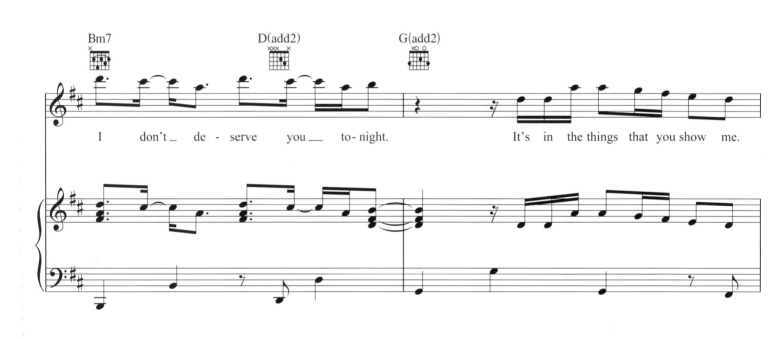

I don't __ de - serve you __ to - night.

It's in the things that you show me.

Sure need you, don't let me go. I need you, don't let me go. I feel like

AS I AM

Words and Music by JUSTIN BIEBER,
GREGORY ERIC HEIN, IDO ZMISHLANY,
SCOTT HARRIS, JOSH GUDWIN,
JORDAN K. JOHNSON, STEFAN JOHNSON,
OLIVER PETERHOF and KHALID DONNEL ROBINSON

OFF MY FACE

Words and Music by JUSTIN BIEBER,
LEAH JAQUELINE PRINGLE, DANIEL JAMES PRINGLE,
TIA SCOLA and JAKE TORREY

HOLY

Words and Music by JUSTIN BIEBER,
JON BELLION, ANTHONY JONES,
TOMMY BROWN, STEVEN FRANKS,
MICHAEL POLLACK, JORGEN ODEGARD
and CHANCELOR BENNETT

* *Recorded a half step lower.*

Em **C** **G** **D/F#**

Can't wait an-oth-er sec-ond 'cause the way you hold me, hold me, hold me, hold me, hold me

1
Em **C**

feels so _____ ho - ly.

2
Em **C**

feels so _____ ho - ly.

G **D/F#** **Em7** **C**

They say we're too young and the pimps and the play-ers say, "Don't go crush-ing."

G **D/F#** **Em7** **C**

Wise men say fools rush in, but I don't ___ know. ___

UNSTABLE

Words and Music by JUSTIN BIEBER,
BILLY WALSH, DELACEY, JOSHUA GUDWIN,
RAMI YACOUB, JAMES GUTCH,
GREGORY HEIN and CHARLTON HOWARD

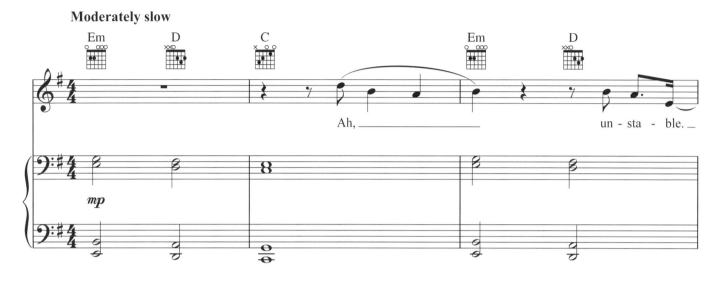

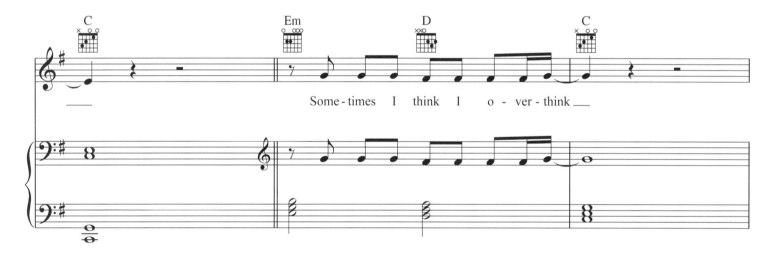

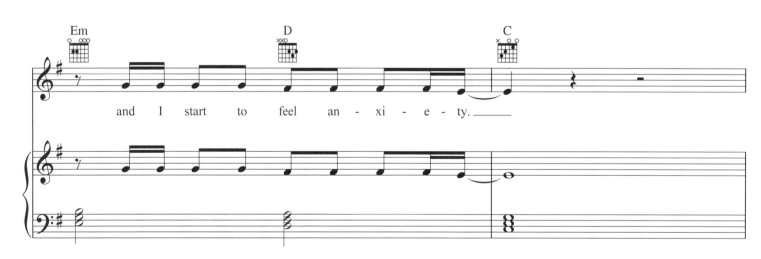

DIE FOR YOU

Words and Music by JUSTIN BIEBER,
JONATHAN BELLION, LOUIS BELL,
ALI TAMPOSI, ANDREW WATT
and DOMINIC DAVID FIKE

* Recorded a half step higher.

D.S. al Coda

HOLD ON

Words and Music by JUSTIN BIEBER,
JON BELLION, ANDREW WATT,
WALTER DE BACKER, ALI TAMPOSI,
LUIZ BONFA and LOUIS BELL

SOMEBODY

Words and Music by JUSTIN BIEBER,
SONNY MOORE, RAMI YACOUB,
JOSH GUDWIN, BERNARD HARVEY,
ILYA SALMANZADEH, RYAN TEDDER
and GREGORY HEIN

GHOST

Words and Music by JUSTIN BIEBER,
JONATHAN BELLION, JORDAN JOHNSON,
STEFAN JOHNSON and MICHAEL POLLACK

Young blood thinks there's al - ways to - mor - row.
Young blood thinks there's al - ways to - mor - row.

I miss your touch on nights ___ when I'm hol - low.
Need more time, but time ___ can't be bor - rowed.

60

PEACHES

Words and Music by JUSTIN BIEBER,
BERNARD HARVEY, LOUIS BELL,
FELISHA KING, ASHTON SIMMONDS,
ANDREW WATT, GIVEON EVANS
and LUIZ MANUEL MARTINEZ Jr.

Dm7   Cmaj7

mo - wa. _____ I got my peach - es out in

Fmaj7   Em7

Geor - gia. (Oh yeah, shit.) I get my weed from Cal - i - for - nia. (That's that shit.) I took my chick up to the

Dm7   Cmaj7

north, yeah. (Bad-ass bitch.) I get my light right from the source, yeah. (Yeah that's it.) I get the feel-ing so I'm

Fmaj7   Em7

sure.   Hand in my hand be-cause I'm yours.   I can't, ___ I can't pre-tend I can't ig-

north, yeah. (Bad-ass bitch.) I get my light right from the source, yeah. (Yeah, that's it.) I got my peach-es out in

Geor-gia. (Oh yeah, shit.) I get my weed from Cal - i - for - nia. (That's that shit.) I took my chick up to the

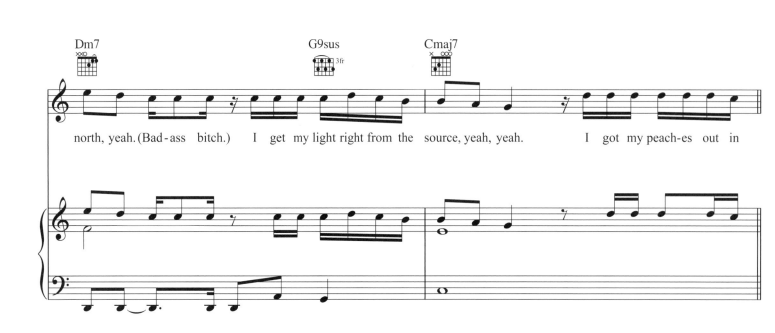

north, yeah. (Bad-ass bitch.) I get my light right from the source, yeah, yeah. I got my peach-es out in

LOVE YOU DIFFERENT

Words and Music by JUSTIN BIEBER,
ALEXANDER IZQUIERDO, OLIVER PETERHOF,
MARCUS LOMAX, WHITNEY PHILLIPS,
TYSHANE THOMPSON and JORDAN DOUGLAS

Recorded a half step higher.

by my side.   You mix the col - or, col - or, col - or, ___ col - or, see the

fu - ture ___ bright.   This is mu - tual, it's not u - sual: ___ when

I'm a - round you I, ___ I,...   Them

goose - bumps, ___ them goose - bumps. ___ The truth hurt, ___ and you know ___ a

LOVED BY YOU

Words and Music by JUSTIN BIEBER,
DAMINI EBUNOLUWA OGULU, JONATHAN BELLION,
JASON EVIGAN, SONNY MOORE and AMY ALLEN

Moderately, in 2

Lyrics:

I bought a cas-tle in France and it's the same one I built __ in the sand for __ you when I __ was two. __

* *Recorded a half step lower.*

LONELY

Words and Music by JUSTIN BIEBER,
BENJAMIN LEVIN and FINNEAS O'CONNELL

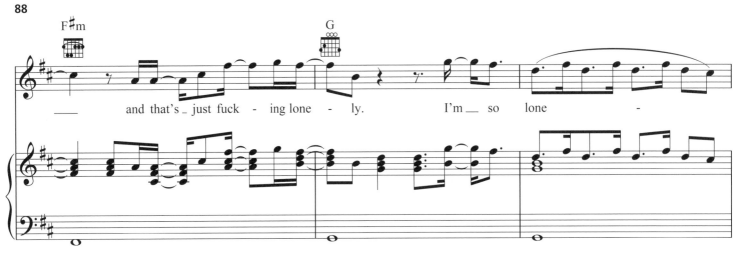

and that's _ just fuck - ing lone - ly. I'm _ so lone -

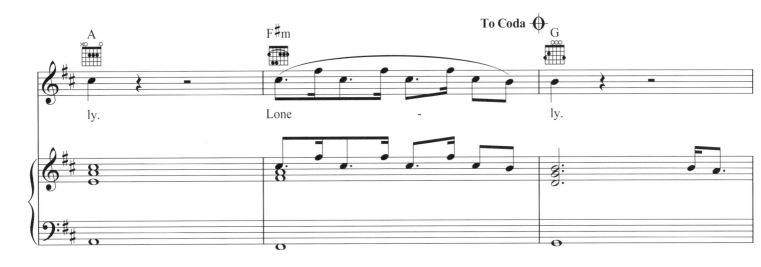

ly. Lone - ly.

Ev - 'ry - bod - y knows my past now, __ like my house was al - ways made of glass. __

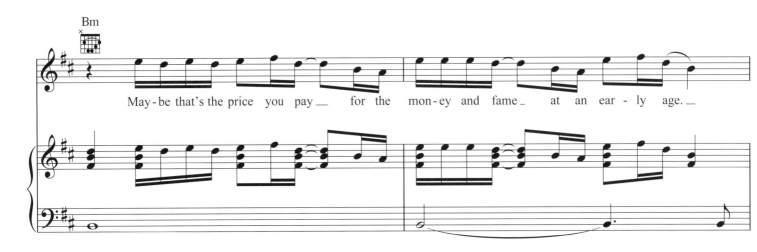

May - be that's the price you pay __ for the mon - ey and fame _ at an ear - ly age. __

ANYONE

Words and Music by JUSTIN BIEBER,
JON BELLION, JORDAN JOHNSON,
ALEXANDER IZQUIERDO, ANDREW WATT,
RAUL CUBINA, STEFAN JOHNSON
and MICHAEL POLLACK

Moderate Pop

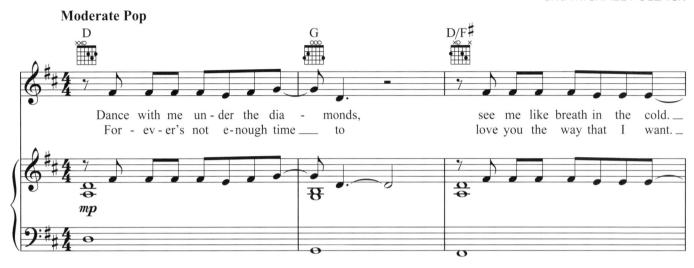

Dance with me un-der the dia - monds, see me like breath in the cold.
For - ev-er's not e-nough time ___ to love you the way that I want. ___

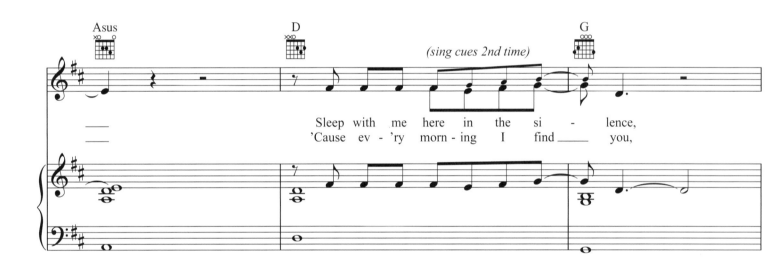

(sing cues 2nd time)

Sleep with me here in the si - lence,
'Cause ev -'ry morn - ing I find ___ you,

come kiss me sil - ver and gold. ___ You say that I won't lose you, but you can't
I fear the day that I don't. ___ You say that I won't lose you, but you can't

More Songbooks from Your Favorite Artists

ADELE – 25

22 songs: All I Ask • Hello – I Miss You • Million Years Ago • River Lea • Send My Love (To Your New Lover) • Water Under the Bridge • When We Were Young • and more.

00155393 Piano/Vocal/Guitar $19.99

SARA BAREILLES – AMIDST THE CHAOS

12 songs: Armor • Fire • No Such Thing • Poetry by Dead Men • A Safe Place to Land (feat. John Legend) • Saint Honesty • and more.

00294277 Piano/Vocal/Guitar $19.99

LEWIS CAPALDI – DIVINELY UNINSPIRED TO A HELLISH EXTENT

Bruises • Don't Get Me Wrong • Fade • Forever • Grace • Headspace • Hold Me While You Wait • Hollywood • Lost on You • Maybe • One • Someone You Loved.

00299905 Piano/Vocal/Guitar $19.99

COLDPLAY – EVERYDAY LIFE

16 tracks featuring the title track plus: Arabesque • Broken • Champion of the World • Church • Cry Cry Cry • Daddy • Eko • Guns • Sunrise • When I Need a Friend • and more.

00327962 Piano/Vocal/Guitar $19.99

BILLIE EILISH – WHEN WE ALL FALL ASLEEP, WHERE DO WE GO?

13 songs: All the Good Girls Go to Hell • Bad Guy • Bury a Friend • 8 • Goodbye • I Love You • ilomilo • Listen Before I Go • My Strange Addiction • When the Party's Over • Wish You Were Gay • Xanny • You Should See Me in a Crown.

00295684 Piano/Vocal/Guitar $19.99

ARIANA GRANDE – THANK U, NEXT

11 songs: Bad Idea • Bloodline • Break up with Your Girlfriend, I'm Bored • Fake Smile • Ghostin • Imagine • In My Head • Make Up • NASA • Needy • 7 Rings.

00292769 Piano/Vocal/Guitar $19.99

LIZZO – CUZ I LOVE YOU

12 songs: Better in Color • Crybaby • Cuz I Love You • Exactly How I Feel • Heaven Help Me • Jerome • Juice • Like a Girl • Lingerie • Soulmate • Tempo • Truth Hurts.

00304758 Piano/Vocal/Guitar $19.99

THE LUMINEERS – III

13 songs: April • Democracy • Donna • Gloria • It Wasn't Easy to Be Happy for You • Jimmy Sparks • Leader of the Landslide • Left for Denver • Life in the City • My Cell • Old Lady • Salt and the Sea • Soundtrack Song.

00322983 Piano/Vocal/Guitar $19.99

SHAWN MENDES

14 songs: Because I Had You • Fallin' All in You • In My Blood • Like to Be You • Lost in Japan • Mutual • Nervous • Particular Taste • Perfectly Wrong • Queen • When You're Ready, I'm Waiting • Where Were You in the Morning? • Why • Youth.

00279536 Piano/Vocal/Guitar $17.99

HARRY STYLES – FINE LINE

12 songs: Adore You • Canyon Moon • Cherry • Falling • Fine Line • Golden • Lights Up • She • Sunflower, Vol. 6 • To Be So Lonely • Treat People with Kindness • Watermelon Sugar.

00338558 Piano/Vocal/Guitar $19.99

TAYLOR SWIFT – FOLKLORE

17 songs: Betty • Cardigan • Exile (feat. Bon Iver) • Illicit Affairs • The Lakes • The Last Great American Dynasty • Mad Woman • The 1 • Peace • and more.

00356804 Piano/Vocal/Guitar $19.99

HAL•LEONARD®

For a complete listing of the products available,
visit us online at **www.halleonard.com**

Contents, prices, and availability subject to change without notice.

0920
015